PORTFOLIO 12

METROPOLITAN SEMINARS IN ART

Portfolio 12 · *The Artist*

by John Canaday

CHIEF OF THE DIVISION OF EDUCATION

THE PHILADELPHIA MUSEUM OF ART

THE METROPOLITAN MUSEUM OF ART

THE ARTIST
The Artist as a Visionary

THIS IS our final portfolio in a series of twelve discussions intended to offer an introduction to the understanding of pictures. We have suggested several answers to the question "What is a painting?" asked in the first portfolio. We have defined realism, expressionism, and abstraction and have offered enough examples of each to indicate that the variation and overlapping of each classification may be infinite. We have analyzed pictorial composition as pattern, as structure, and as a relationship of forms determined by special problems of expression. We have seen that the various techniques, besides being the means of getting pigment to adhere to a surface in a satisfactory manner, are in themselves elements of expression.

If the discussions have succeeded in their purpose, then anyone who has followed them should have found new ways of looking at pictures to discover within them some meanings not apparent on the surface. But it should also be clear by now that not many pictures follow a formula without modifying it, at least not many very good pictures and hardly any great ones. For the artist formula must always take second place to invention; this means that for the observer formula must always take second place to perception. These discussions have tried to explain general principles and to give some kind of basis for the speedier development of individual perception. The pictures discussed—about 150 of them—were chosen because they were suitable points of departure for the understanding of many others, but even in these key pictures it is true that the subtlest meaning in each is distinctive to itself. In the end a picture is a personal communication with the observer, in which a guide or interpreter is only in the way.

We have called these discussions an introduction to painting, but all acquaintance with painting is an introduction to it since each new painting is a new experience. If by a miracle it were possible for one person to have universal knowledge of painting up to this moment, everything he knew would be only an introduction to the pictures that will be painted tomorrow, whether those pictures are good or bad, false or sincere, conventional or revolutionary. Art is so various that once we have begun its exploration we are always in midstream.

Since we have been engaged in something like a course of study, it might seem reasonable to devote this last portfolio to an exposition of some knottier problems than any we have tackled so far, basing the explanations on what we have learned from the preceding pictures. But this would suggest that the understanding of painting depends more than it does on the application of rules and systems. This portfolio will be concerned, instead, with some pictures that are essentially unexplainable in any specific sense. Their subjects are visionary, fantastic, grotesque, or mystical—hence they depend to the utmost on that communication between picture and observer that may be facilitated by rules and general principles but is finally determined by the unique reaction of the individual to a unique image.

Giorgione's *The Tempest* (Plate 133) is—partly by accident—a perfect example of such a picture because, though its original meaning has been lost, it is so provocative to the imagination that it must have meaning for anyone with a grain of perception. The meaning must be entirely personal; the title is an arbitrary one since we have no idea what Giorgione originally called it. (It is also sometimes called *Soldier and Gypsy*, a title that presumes more than we can actually know about the two figures.) It is beautifully composed; its individual elements are in themselves quite irrational and contradictory, yet they are integrated into a perfectly unified whole.

To one side of the picture a young woman suckles a child. She is nude except for a length of cloth draped across her shoulders. Her attitude is not particularly one of maternal tenderness; she seems rather to be engaged in some casual, undefinable reverie (*Figure 1*). Her presence in the countryside upon this grassy bank, amid luxuriant sprays and clumps of foliage, is unexplained yet appears inevitable. She seems unaware of the other figure or of the gathering storm; although she glances in our direction, she does so without any response to our presence. It is important to the extraordinary impression of isolation created around her that she is separated from us by a delicate filigree of leaves and branches springing from the rock in the immediate foreground.

The figure on the opposite side is a very young man, hardly more than an adolescent, sometimes described as a knight, sometimes as a shepherd, who carries a staff that is not quite appropriate to either. The figure is graceful and assured, alert in contrast to the half-meditative, half-enchanted young woman. He regards her attentively, and his position in the extreme foreground and his graceful pose suggest an awareness of the observer. He is the only element that invites our participation in the picture. We are barely admitted to the right foreground, and we are fenced out of the left, as soon as we have encompassed the figure of the youth, by a barrier of foliage, water, and architectural ruins, beyond which some buildings of a town or city rise in spectral illumination against a dark sky breached by a vivid streak of lightning.

Giorgione, a Venetian, painted *The Tempest* about 1508. It is typical of Venetian renaissance painting in its transmutation of sensuous luxury into pastoral idyllicism. In Giorgione's other paintings and in works by his contemporaries we find the same combination of soft golden flesh, tender foliage, gleaming velvets and satins, mellowed stones, the same sense of the touch of air, the same glowing lights and vibrant shadows. They are all present, for instance, in Giorgione's *The Concert (Figure 2)*. *The Concert* is a compound expression of the delights of the flesh and the senses that rises above salaciousness or vulgarity because it is conceived in the spirit of pagan worship of sensuous delight rather than commonplace indulgence.

The Tempest and *The Concert* may originally have been conceived in much the same spirit; in both of them, certainly, there is the same sensuous delight. The great difference between them is that in *The Concert* our curiosity is satisfied by the completeness we find in the picture. Its greatness lies there, in the fullness of its statement. But the fascination of *The Tempest* is increased by the element of mystery arising from its lost subject. Some day the subject may be discovered. Various explanations have been suggested. It may be an illustration for a lost poem. Some historians believe it illustrates an episode from an ancient Greek story. Or perhaps it is an allegory, an explanation that would account for the curious combination of figures and objects and would

Figure 1

change the picture from a poetic mystery into a didactic exercise.

Nothing, of course, could quite do that. No explanation, however precise and irrefutable, could transform *The Tempest* from a poetic masterpiece into a collection of arbitrary symbols. For the poetry does not lie in the objects themselves nor does the mystery lie entirely in the strangeness of their combination. It is their unification as forms in light and their harmony as sensuous experiences that lift this collection of miscellaneous and itemizable objects to the level of an experience not to be explained in terms of the world. It would not be proper or safe to wonder whether *The Tempest* is a more expressive picture for having lost its subject. But it is probably a different picture. Its details remain explicit while the total statement Giorgione intended them to make remains mysterious, so that its meaning is of necessity a matter of personal response to all the suggestions involved. *The Tempest* may have begun as an allegory; it has become a dream. When we look at it the dream becomes our own, and our own interpretation of it becomes the legitimate one.

The Imagery of Dream

What is the image of a dream? By popular conception it is fuzzy, misty, half-formed, and wavering—no doubt because of the quickness with which dreams fade from memory and their elusiveness when we try to describe them. But in actual experience a dream may be, and usually is, acutely vivid. When painters have set about exploring this otherworld they have usually chosen to do so in forms of exceptional clarity, sharper than reality, so that the fantasy and unreality of the visionary forms are intensified.

William Blake, the eighteenth-century English painter and poet whose *Wise and Foolish Virgins* was discussed as a composition in Portfolio 5, wrote: "A spirit and a vision are not, as the modern philosophers suppose, a cloudy vapour or a nothing; they are organized and minutely articulated beyond all that the mortal and perishable nature can produce. He who does not imagine in stronger and better lineaments and in stronger and better light than his perishing and mortal eye can see, does not imagine at all."

Blake's "perishing and mortal eye" was frequently indistinguishable from his imagination. At the age of four he told his parents that he had seen God's head at the window, an incident frequently related to indicate his visionary nature but one common enough in children at that age. But at the age of seven his vision of the prophet Ezekiel in the fields surrounded by angels in trees was more exceptional. The wings of the angels were "bespangling the boughs like stars." Even if this description, as quoted much later by his wife, has the benefit of hindsight, it is quite in the spirit of Blake's art and temper. From his wife, too, we have the description of Blake's death, certainly as jubilant a passing as has ever been recorded. He was seventy years old and confined to bed, where he worked on a set of drawings illustrating Dante. On the day of his death he called his wife and told her, "Kate, you have been a good wife; I will draw your portrait." He proceeded to do so for an hour as she sat by the window and then, according to her account, "he began to sing Hallelujahs and songs of joy and triumph, loudly and with ecstatic energy. His bursts of gladness made the walls resound," and then he died. This was a man who had suffered poverty and scorn and had been forced to live on the thinly disguised charity of friends.

Like so many artists of extreme individuality Blake must be accepted without question or completely rejected. His paintings and engravings are ecstatic and thrilling visions, or they are conscientious but obvious and labored illustrations based on forms cribbed from Raphael and Michelangelo. In everything Blake did, his naïveté is a primary characteristic. In *The Archangel Raphael with Adam and Eve* (Plate 134) there is not the slightest question that Adam and Eve are two specific human beings of exceptional beauty (as Blake conceived of human beauty, in terms of renaissance idealizations). They are receiving instructions from the angel Raphael in a Garden of Eden where twining plants and exotic trees of Blake's own invention are as real as his own small garden where he was fond of impersonating, or of confusing himself and his wife with, Adam and Eve. To Blake the word "real" described what was most real to him, whether it was of this world or another world. He appears to have made little distinction between the world around him—at least, that part of it which he was willing to accept—

and the world of the Bible, Milton, Dante, and Shakespeare. The world he synthesized in his art drew from all these sources. He might have admired Giorgione's *The Tempest* as an unexplained vision, but he would have scorned it as an explained allegory—that, for him, would have turned it into nothing but a charade. "Fable or allegory is a totally distinct and inferior kind of poetry," he wrote. "Vision or Imagination is a representation of what actually exists real and unchangeably." That for him there existed no boundary between tangible fact and visionary fabrication brings Blake close to lunacy by definition. He might indeed have ended as a confined lunatic if his wife had not combined unquestioning faith in his appointed role as a spiritual messenger

The Louvre Museum, Paris; photo by Archives Photographiques

Figure 2

9

with an un-Blakean capacity for holding body and soul together. Kate has achieved her own special immortality in the history of art.

Blake's water colors and, of course, his engravings retain the strong lineaments in which he created them, but his tempera paintings have deteriorated to such a degree that some of them have turned to the "cloudy vapour" that so offended him as the conception of a dream or a vision. He used some form of glue tempera of his own concoction that has deteriorated badly, with much crackling and discoloration. Yet the effect is not altogether unpleasant nor does it obscure the forms in paintings like *Zacharias and the Angel* (*Figure 3*). Apparently in his temperas the forms were originally even more substantial than in his water colors, even if they were not quite so sharply delineated. *Zacharias and the Angel* is filled with flame and light and smoke, filled with a spreading brilliance now visible through and exaggerated by the veil of crackling. We can guess that in their original condition these paintings, more than Blake's water colors, combined the conventional effect of apparitions in a miraculous light with the artist's insistence upon a strong and tangible image.

This combination is typical of the art of Redon, who goes further than most visionary painters in the direction of hazy definition. Sometimes, as in his *Evocation of the Butterflies* (*Figure 4*), a soft, wavering iridescence, formless or half-formed, covers the picture area; here even the butterflies scattered across it are only half-defined. Large areas of a painting by Redon may suggest the shifting and transient glimmering of an oil film upon the surface of water. A Redon work may seem to violate Blake's demand for minute articulation in the painting of vision, but it is a mistake to think that a Redon painting is composed in a haphazard or accidental manner or even to think that his forms are altogether insubstantial ones. Redon began as a student of architecture and later worked at sculpture,

two arts in which the physical existence of three-dimensional form is, obviously, basic to the designer's conception. And when Redon said that in his painting he wanted to put "the logic of the visible to the service of the invisible" he was striking close to Blake's idea that organization and articulation are imperative to the creation of images of fantasy.

Redon's *Apollo* (*Figure 5*) bears this out. The god's chariot is drawn through an empyrean of clouds and fire dramatically expressive of flaming space. We are at the opposite pole from Blake's systematic linear rhythms, which carry us with inescapable definition from one point to another and back again over the surface of his picture. But we can apply to a picture like *Apollo* the informal test of any composition: is it possible to change the picture's structure without weakening or transforming its nature? Can we, for instance, cut down the right side, in which nothing happens, change the attitude of any one of the horses, make the chariot and Apollo larger or smaller, make the reins connecting it to the horses more conspicuous or less so? The test could be pushed to the point of absurdity, but in general it is certainly true that the composition is as well articulated as one of Blake's, if less obviously, and that in the end it depends more on formal values than on ambiguous ones in its visionary description.

Dream, Miracle, and Nightmare

Blake's *The Archangel Raphael with Adam and Eve* was painted at the end of the eighteenth century, the age of reason, and Redon's *Apollo* at the beginning of the twentieth, the age of science, so both artists fall outside the major currents of their times. But if we go back to the Middle Ages we enter a period when reason was put into the service of the miraculous, and science was half fantasy. Hieronymus Bosch's *The Garden of Eden* (*Plate 135*) is as

Figure 3

explicit as Blake's and as visionary, but he did not have to theorize about it. Bosch's *Hell* (Plate 135) was quite naturally painted in detail as specific as that of any earthly landscape because hell's existence was accepted, and its horrors could be catalogued and believed by medieval man as easily as we may now believe a guidebook's descriptions of a country we have never seen. The art of the age abounds in fantasies—some of them symbolic, some of them accepted as literal truth, and some of them apparently the result of nothing more profound than a rollicking attraction to the grotesque for its own sake. Cathedral entrances were lined with statues of the saints, surmounted by Last Judgments, Resurrections, or Ascensions, and encrusted with the miraculous Christian story materialized into stone figures of unquestionable reality. And higher up on these buildings

clustered the gargoyles, fantastic half-diabolic and half-humorous inventions as plausible to the medieval mind as any dog or cat in the streets. In manuscripts like The Hours of Jeanne d'Évreaux (*Figure 6*) these little monsters appear with a kind of gaiety as part of the decorative borders.

Bosch was the most terrifying of the medieval painters of the fantastic. He worked at the end of the Middle Ages, when the conviction of sin was stronger in the human spirit than the conviction of grace. In discussing realism we described the infinite detail of Van Eyck's *Saint Francis Receiving the Stigmata* (Plate 16, Portfolio 2) and said that its microscopic description of natural objects took on spiritual meaning through the medieval conception that every particle of matter in the world, no matter how small, was inherently significant because all existence was part of an

11

orderly scheme created by the will of God.

In Bosch's fantasies this conception is reversed. He creates a universe as detailed as Van Eyck's, but it explores the depths of sin and evil and the damnation of the soul. Detail by detail he paints as explicitly and as naturalistically as Van Eyck; we recognize in his hellish figures parts of plants or machines or birds or animals, but these naturalistic parts are combined into an outlandish and horrifying whole. Their horror comes from the incontrovertible existence of these monsters. They are true. Like Redon, Bosch puts "the logic of the visible to the service of the invisible," and, as Blake wanted to do, he organizes and articulates his inventions into something more vivid than the "perishing and mortal eye" can see.

The Garden of Eden and *Hell* (Plate 135) are the left and right panels of a triptych. The wings tell respectively of man's creation in innocence and of his consequent damnation. *The Garden of Eden*, where we see the creation of Eve, is like Blake's in showing against

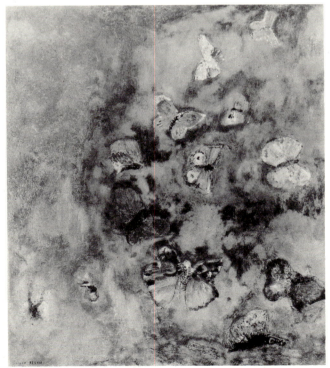

The Detroit Institute of Arts

Figure 4

distant crags an exotic garden where the animals of the earth wander at peace with one another. But whereas Blake's invention is gentle and trusting, Bosch's has variety and force. The prophecy of evil in Blake's garden is made by an out-size tree in the distance around which the serpent is coiled. In Bosch's it is present in a subtler and more ominous way, in the suggestion of evil taken on by the monstrously unnatural forms of the foliage, the fountain, and the crags, and by the sinister shapes and activities of some of the animals, which are like spots of infection in the terrestrial paradise.

The large central panel shows *The Garden of Earthly Delights* (*Figure 7*). The pleasures of the flesh are extolled, but with full consciousness of the medieval connotations of the sinfulness of fleshly indulgence. At virtually the same time, in the more relaxed moral climate of Venice, Giorgione was able to transmute these pleasures into the idyllic reveries of *The Tempest* and *The Concert*, as we have just seen. But Bosch's *Garden of Earthly Delights* is a nightmarish circus where swarms of lissome naked bodies are compounded with evil grotesqueries.

In the third panel, *Hell*, all delights are abandoned in a vision of pure evil where logic and illogic are indistinguishable from one another. Although this is a hell where some physical tortures take place, these tortures are the smallest part of a hell where the real torture is spiritual, where corruptions, deformities, monstrous growths, mutilations, and agonizing transformations are the norm. The damned soul is wracked less by physical pain than by its existence in a world where all reason and order have been grotesquely transmuted by some cancerous misdirection of divine order.

In a detail from *Hell* (Plate 136) the head of the central figure, that concoction of parts that must be called "figure" for want of any other word, has by legend been called Bosch's own portrait. This figure looks back over its—can

Figure 5

we say shoulder?—from beneath a disk that suggests a hatbrim. Resting on the disk is a bladderlike form terminating in a musical pipe and a spout from which issues smoke and flame. This whole invention is surrounded, in turn, by demons leading naked, condemned souls by the hand, round and round. Whether or not the head is Bosch's portrait, its sly, half-demonic, acutely observant air suggests his spirit. This head grows from a huge eggshell-like body, hollow and broken open at one end, supported by leglike growths. They stand in two small, rigged boats and branch into the form of blasted trees with dead, pointed limbs that grow upward to pierce the body, whose hollow interior is occupied by tiny figures engaged in a variety of activities.

In every fragment—and a Bosch is cumulatively effective as it is examined fragment by fragment—we are presented with a specific and concrete image of a hell-form whose reality and whose impossibility are equally undeniable until, like the condemned souls themselves, we are taken up by the force of unreason. Occasionally the figures of this mad-normal world are hideously comical. The little bird-headed, pig-tailed demon walking near the front edge of the "hatbrim" carrying a burning staff is such a one. These not-really-humorous figures are as horrifying as the more obviously monstrous ones; the humor is as devilish as the tortures.

Among Bosch's several followers or imitators was Pieter Huys. Although his pictorial

13

Figure 6

Contrastingly, Huys shows the saint within a crowded nightmarescape centering around the lovely figure of a nude girl but flowering all round into evil forms. The girl holds a small owl (always a witchlike bird, associated with things dark and ominous), while behind her crouches a hag with a distaff and beside her a female monster with a platter upon which she offers what appears to be a piece of carrion. To describe the picture further would be only to continue an enumeration of the hideous inventions that torment the holy man. The harmonious serenity of Sassetta's conception of the subject and the agonized complications of Huys's are offered here as a reminder of one of our opening definitions of what a picture is: a reflection of the personality of the man who painted it and an expression of the time and place that produced it. The contrast lies particularly between the premise that dominates Italian painting, that in spite of its evils the world ultimately is good, orderly, and beautiful, and the Northern one, that in spite of its joys and diversions the world is basically tragic, malevolent, and mysterious.

The Devil in the Twentieth Century

The world we have seen in Bosch and Huys is disturbing because it operates within a set of irrational laws to which we are subject when we enter their pictures. Jumping forward four and a half centuries and substituting Freudian theory for biblical prophecies of hell-fire and damnation, we enter the world of the twentieth-century surrealist painters, which operates in much the same way. The sinful hallucinations besetting Saint Anthony in his wilderness are the Freudian dreams of anybody anywhere today; from them the surrealists have created a nightmareworld that borrows heavily from the earlier painters. The agonized creature rending itself in Salvador Dali's *Soft Construction with Boiled Beans*

concoctions do not approach those of the master in hellish power, he is worth a parenthetical reference here to compare his *Temptation of Saint Anthony* (*Figure 8*) with Sassetta's treatment of the same subject, *Saint Anthony Tempted by the Devil* (Plate 78, Portfolio 7), which might also have been included in this portfolio for its dreamlike quality.

The Temptation of Saint Anthony was a rich subject for the painters of diableries; Bosch himself did a large picture of this hermit saint whose mind was a battleground between his yearning to achieve grace through prayer and meditation and the evil thoughts that obsessed him. Sassetta reduced the story to its essentials: the symbol of temptation (the woman), the symbol of meditation (the hut), the dreamlike wilderness where the drama takes place, and the saint himself.

14

Figure 7

(*Figure 9*) is obviously a relative of the eggshell figure from Bosch's *Hell*. And the same surrealist painter's *Apparition of Face and Fruit Dish on a Beach* (Plate 137) is an even more curious kind of dream or nightmare picture.

Apparition is, among other things, an exercise in the invention of double images. We are all familiar with the shifting and changing of the subjects of our dreams: "I was in our old house, in the living room, and then all of a sudden it seemed to be a cave instead. There were a lot of people there, and I didn't seem to recognize them, but at the same time I realized they were all people we know."

15

Figure 8

Just so, in *Apparition* the foreground is a smooth beach that changes imperceptibly into a table covered with a cloth. The apparition of the head fuses with that of a compote full of fruit—a variation on the Boschian device in which a single figure is a composite of animal, vegetable, and mineral forms—and combines, too, with objects on the shore such as the jar that does double duty as an eye. The upper right quarter of the picture is a technically exquisite landscape, crowded with inventions of corruption and decay, stretching back into a distance of magical clarity where peaks rise against the enameled sky. But with a sudden reversal of scale and meaning this landscape becomes a dog's head; a tunnel becomes his eye, and a viaduct his studded collar. The animal's body merges into the apparitional fruit dish, and his hindquarters are suggested

in the odd shape rising at the far left. A length of frayed rope and a bit of discarded cloth lying on the beach complete the picture. Perhaps these last have an obscure and personal symbolism for the painter himself. Perhaps, one suspects, they are there as a demonstration of his technical dexterity as much as anything else.

This suspicion of exhibitionism by the artist is the flaw in surrealism and constitutes the difference between its purportedly visionary nature and that of someone like Bosch. There is a feeling that the synthesis of forms is arbitrary and tricky, whereas Bosch's combinations are purposeful. One reason is that the surrealists, particularly the one who painted this picture, have indulged in so much conspicuous zaniness that their art has become suspect with much of the public. As a matter

16

of fact, sensationalism and shock are inherent in surrealism. Their use is conscious, open, and hence legitimate up to a point. The surrealist painter may theoretically indulge in behavior that is undignified, eccentric, or outrageous by conventional standards and yet be acting within his credo. The trouble is that this liberty has so often been extended to include publicity stunts that the lay public has difficulty in regarding surrealism as a serious and thoughtful art. (Nor is it always; no "ism" has been more prostituted.) The most generous attitude to take toward the more bizarre novelties of the surrealists is to consider that like most modern painting surrealism is an intensely personal expression and as such cannot be expected to achieve the same force as the art of Bosch, who worked at a time when painting was an expression of great unified social forces rather than a purely personal response to isolated and specialized fragments of social experience.

Before leaving *Apparition*, we may point out that Blume's *The Eternal City* in the preceding portfolio has certain connections with surrealist techniques that are unexpected in a painting in which the comment is sociopolitical. But if it is surprising, it is not nearly so surprising as the general resurgence of fantastic art in this century. This is the age that has made a fetish of science, yet our painters have been more prolific and varied in exploring the worlds of pure imagination than any painters since the Middle Ages, when the otherworld was a part of daily life. Blake was all but alone in his time as a visionary painter, and his audience was small. Our fantasts inhabit even more private worlds than his, and their audience is wide and receptive. The references in the art of Marc Chagall, as in *Birthday* (*Figure 10*), are quite personal; they speak of his life as a boy in Russia, stories of which he has been fond, his love and marriage, anything that gives him delight. If ever a man painted for himself alone, Chagall did. His typical painting is a private (and very happy) reverie

Figure 9

that he makes no effort to explain. It may be that the world being too much with us these days we are especially glad to be taken out of it for a while, and that painters, for the same reason, find satisfaction in leaving this world for excursions into one of their own invention.

The Logic of Dream

Giorgio de Chirico created one of the first of these invented worlds and one of the most enduring. Before the word surrealism was invented he anticipated many of its devices, minus its morbidity and its sensationalism. Again and again he painted combinations and recombinations of a limited set of motives that, for all their repetition from picture to picture, retain undiminished their sense of mystery and melancholy touched with an ominous foreboding but mitigated by a pervading serenity. The world he creates is at once desolate and intimate, empty but filled with suggestion, deserted, yet full of mysterious presences, a world that is never explained and possibly for that very reason never palls.

The elements in *Melancholy and Mystery of a Street* (*Figure 11*), for instance, and those in *The Anguish of Departure* (Plate 138) overlap,

17

Figure 10

and both pictures overlap others, yet each is individual. In the same way realistic landscapes may be individual though composed of the same set of elements—trees, hills, sky, and the other usual features. The collective mood of Chirico's dreamscapes is suggested by the titles he gives them. In addition to melancholy and mystery, anguish and departure, the titles repeat such words as serenity, surprise, lassitude, enigma, delight and joy, destiny and uncertainty, torment and dream, nostalgia and return. The words scholar, philosopher, and poet are also frequent; soothsaying and metaphysics and fatality have their visual counterparts in Chirico's repetitions of long arcades in unyielding perspective, statues in

deserted squares, tiny distant figures dwarfed by their own extended shadows, towers, great isolated smokestacks, huge boxes, and wheeled vans unattended and unexplained.

The van in *Melancholy and Mystery of a Street* is empty. What was in it? Or what is it waiting to receive? In *The Anguish of Departure* the van doors are closed. What do they hide? We cannot rationalize the presence of the van nor the disposition and relationship of any of the objects in a Chirico painting on any kind of logical basis, yet their existence is very real. The words "irrefutable logic" are familiar; in Chirico's dreamscapes there is something like an irrefutable *illogic* that accounts for the harmonious existence to-

18

gether in the picture of so many contradictory elements, at once so disturbing and so serene.

Chirico wrote that a painting should bring to the observer the "sensation of something new," something he had never known before. He wrote that "the strange sensations which a man can experience, faithfully reproduced by this man, can always give new joys to a sensitive and intelligent person." We are not to suppose that Chirico experienced in dream the images he reproduces for us. His inventions, born of his own temperament and perceptions, give visual existence to inner experiences of his own that we thus may share.

Of course we are always sharing in this way when we enjoy painting. In Chirico's case the difference lies in the extremely personal nature of the experience, so personal that some people may be offended by the idea of understanding and sharing an experience that seems to them abnormal and outlandish. It is quite possible that the feeling of antagonism to much modern art is the result of just this reaction on the part of many people. The answer to such antagonism is simply that there is no obligation on anyone's part to share an experience he would rather reject or one he is incapable of absorbing.

However, anyone who has trouble entering Chirico's world, but wants to, should be able to approach it through an intermediary, Chirico's early teacher, Arnold Böcklin. Böcklin's *Island of the Dead* (Plate 139), painted in 1880, has been a tremendously popular picture, though it is just now at the awkward age that comes to so many paintings a generation or so after their first success, when they look a little old-fashioned and are unnecessarily abused by critics who seem to resent their former success. And certainly in much of his work Böcklin's efforts at fantasy seem heavy-handed, as in *The Triton and the Neriad* (*Figure 12*), where his power of invention is limited to adding fins, fishtails, and seaweed to some exceptionally unattractive models. But our concern is with his more successful

Island of the Dead and its value as an approach to Chirico. It is easier to understand than a Chirico painting because it probes less deeply into otherworldliness. This island is one whose actual existence is easy to imagine in terms of this world, in terms of familiar experience. Somber and spectral it may be, but it could be created in hard fact, given a rocky island of adequate size and an adequate body of water. It would not be difficult to pose costumed figures in a boat just as Böcklin has painted them here. In an evening light the scene would take on an appropriately eerie quality, especially if we happened to know that the island was a cemetery (just as we must know the title of the picture for it to make its full effect). Watching from the bank, as in essence we do when we stand in front of the painting, we might be stirred to certain thoughts of life, death, and afterlife, presumably the thoughts Böcklin intends to stir in us by creating for us a scene that never existed except as he invented it but that actually could exist, literally and concretely. Even the most practical down-to-

Mr. and Mrs. Stanley R. Resor

Figure 11

19

Bayerische Staatsgemäldesammlungen, Munich

Figure 12

The Metropolitan Museum of Art

Figure 13

earth person can exercise his imagination sufficiently to enter into the very slight exaggerations and deceptions Böcklin permits himself in *Island of the Dead.*

But Chirico's dreamscapes could never be re-created, any more than could Bosch's monstrous spectacles. No such light has ever illuminated the objects of this world; the laws of optics do not permit such curious perspectives. Even more importantly, the eye, left to its own devices, would never select, modify, or exaggerate among the visible objects as Chirico dictates that it must do when he lightens or darkens an outline or employs any other of the innumerable devices available to the creator of imaginary objects but denied the imitator of actual ones. For all these reasons Chirico should be able to bring us a more rewarding experience than Böcklin. In responding to Chirico we travel in the same direction that we are taken by Böcklin, but we travel further, explore more deeply, and enter a new world instead of remaining within theatrical modifications of this one.

Böcklin was a late follower of the nineteenth-century romantic movement that flared up early in the century as a revolt against the desiccating official painting. The emotionalization of romantic painting stretched over a gamut of sensitivities ranging from lyricism to violence. We have seen two of the great romantics in Géricault (*The Raft of the Medusa*, Plate 71, Portfolio 6) and Delacroix (*The Abduction of Rebecca*, Plate 72, Portfolio 6). *The Raft of the Medusa* is a melodrama based on a contemporary event, and the emotion of *The Abduction of Rebecca* is more intellectualized than spontaneous, so that neither picture can be called visionary in the sense of the pictures we have been examining in this portfolio. But the romantic spirit, which obviously moves in the direction of visionary expression, produced some remarkable pictures of the kind we can call dreamscapes. These may appear unexpectedly, like passages of dream breaking through the more pedestrian course of a work.

Museum of Fine Arts, Boston

Figure 14

Dream within Reality

One American of the period, Washington Allston, is notable in this respect. Like any aspiring provincial artist he tended to follow established formulas in his most ambitious compositions, with the usual result that they are a little forced and pretentious. But his natural bent was for visionary expression. The works he thought of as minor are the ones that now do him most credit. His famous *Deluge* (*Figure 13*), painted in 1804 during a stay in Paris, is a fine romantic conception done fifteen years before Géricault sounded the battlecry of the romantic movement in the Salon of 1819 with *The Raft of the Medusa*. But in a less ambitious effort, painted thirty years later in his own America, Allston created spontaneously, apparently without being aware that he was doing so, a picture with the true quality of dream. He gave it the long factual title of *Landscape, American Scenery: Time, Afternoon, with a Southwest Haze* (*Figure 14*), indicating an intention to reproduce specifically the look of a certain place under certain conditions. But by the evidence of the picture itself, he was painting from some deep inner experience. However specific the source of the picture may have been, it has little to do with one time or one place. Instead it becomes, with its horse and rider moving alone and silent through some golden otherworld, a vision of the isolation of the human spirit in a region beyond time and beyond place.

The first half of the nineteenth century in America produced some of the most poetically evocative paintings of the century anywhere. As in the case of Allston's work, they are likely to have a touch of awkwardness or naiveté in comparison with their European models, giving them a special quality of their own that is extremely engaging. In his *Flight of Florimell* (Plate 140) Allston was inspired by Venetian painting of the same general type as *The Tempest* and *The Concert*. The foliage of the trees, the gleaming fabric, and the escape into a distant landscape of warm serenity are Venetian. But the special enchantment of *The Flight of Florimell* is its own. Instead of the openness of the Venetian pictures we have a cave of trees into which falls a small pool of golden light. The feeling of seclusion and mysterious isolation is increased because we catch a glimpse of distant landscape through a small windowlike opening through which we may look but not pass. And whatever Allston intended, his slender, delicate-legged horse is motionless, as if magically transfixed, even to the regular waves of its flowing tail—as are the rider and her fluttering scarf. *The Flight of Florimell* happens to illustrate an episode from Spenser, but it is so complete in its own magical suggestion that there is little temptation to attach it to its subject. One is delighted to find in Allston's comments on the Venetians who inspired him that "the poetry of color gives birth to a thousand things which the eye cannot see" and that their pictures "leave the subject to be made by the spectator, provided he possesses the imaginative faculty." This is exactly what happens in *The Flight of Florimell*.

The Flight of Florimell is a fantasy, but the century also produced a group of American painters who, to an exceptional degree, revealed that a dream or a vision need not be shaped in fantasy but may exist in ordinary aspects of the world around us. This is shown in Thomas Cole's *In the Catskills* (Plate 141).

Figure 15

Cole was the leader of the mid-nineteenth-century school of American romantic landscape painters called the Hudson River school. In commenting on one of these pictures, Durand's *Imaginary Landscape* (Plate 7, Portfolio 1), we have noted its preoccupation with the mystery and grandeur of nature, in this instance expressed in terms merging with those of fantastic invention. Cole also paints in these terms some of the time. In one exceptional picture dated 1833, *The Titan's Goblet*, he even anticipated the surrealist device of combining detailed realism with unrealistic reversals of scale. (The goblet holds ships borne upon a vast lake.)

But in *In the Catskills* Cole is less novel and more subtle, revealing the world of dream within the world we know. Without much question the landscape was painted with faithful reference to an actual spot and could still be identified by its topographical features. Lyrical in a way familiar enough in landscape painting, it is more than a competent picture in this respect alone. But when we come close to it and examine it minutely as we do a Bosch or a good surrealist picture we discover something more: spotted in little openings between trees, in small valleys or upon little rises and promontories, and in a section of river emerging from concealing banks and foliage, there are human figures isolated from one another in small, intimate, enclosed worlds. A man chases horses that race through a field (*Figure*

22

15); another rows a boat across the glassy water (*Figure 16*); a hunter approaches a fence (*Figure 17*). Ordinary enough in themselves, each little world-within-a-world grows magical because each is magically revealed. We see them as if gifted with superhuman vision; they are at once close to us and infinitely removed, at once intimate and inaccessible. It is unlikely that the painter held any such end or theory in mind, but that is beside the point. The visions are there; if we want to explain their presence we must suppose that they crystallized from the painter's inmost experience. It is this gift of crystallizing inner experience that differentiates an artist from a mere craftsman or

Figure 16

technician, and sometimes this crystallization takes place through the chemistry of some power unwilled or even unsuspected by the painter.

The most conspicuous manifestation of this power occurs in the art of Henri Rousseau, usually called Douanier Rousseau in reference to his occupation as a customs clerk. He would be called today a hobby painter. He was without professional ambitions of the usual sort, yet he seems never to have doubted for a moment that he was a great painter. He was an extremely simple man in his origins and in his way of life, having a next-to-incredible naiveté. What he wrote about his pictures is often completely at variance with the impression

they make. He would describe as a "genre scene" (that is, a subject from everyday life, realistically treated) a picture full of mystery and enchantment. This quality is peculiarly his own. On the surface he is one of those thousands of untrained "Sunday painters" who create pictures in their spare time for relaxation. His work bears every mark of the conscientious but unskilled beginner. In his *Landscape with Cattle* (Plate 142) we see them all—the flatness of forms intended to appear round, the labored detail, the meticulous but awkward finish, the stiffness, the inaccuracies of proportion and perspective, the trite subject (though a subject is trite only when tritely approached)—in short, the Sunday painting's general air of naiveté, a natural result of technical limitations.

But the picture has something more. It has decorative flair (particularly apparent in the patterning of foliage), a pleasant but superficial virtue, and beyond that it has—inexplicably but irrefutably—an air of enchantment. The flat, rigid objects are transfixed within some magical suspension of time from which every distracting banality has been distilled. Rousseau could not so much as copy a picture postcard (as he sometimes did) without transforming its trite realism into his own distinctive unreality.

Rousseau was fortunate enough to receive from established painters whom he admired

Figure 17

the good advice to avoid formal training even when he was in a position to take advantage of it. Emulating himself, he developed a style of great polish and assurance: he performed the unlikely feat of preserving the fly of his innocence in the amber of his technical sophistication. In pictures like the well-known *The Sleeping Gypsy* (*Figure 18*) exotic subject matter intensifies and makes more obvious the otherworldliness inherent in all his work.

The Innocent Sophisticate

The piquant combination of innocence and sophistication in a single manner is frequent in visionary or fantastic art, but it is seldom so neatly balanced as in Rousseau. Blake, as an instance we have already seen, was first of all an innocent, for all his theories, and the balance between his innocence and the renaissance forms he borrowed to express it is so

precarious that he frequently pushes close to the edge of disharmony. At the other end of this range is Paul Klee, a German-Swiss fantast of the most exquisite sophistication whose painterly vocabulary is adapted from the art of children and savages. Klee's art is immediately comprehensible to some people, never comprehensible to some others, and a mystery to be solved for most. He is not a formula painter, and no formula can explain him. Any understanding must begin with the acceptance of two premises: first, Paul Klee is a highly trained painter of great technical skill and an esthetician of great subtlety and complication, no matter how slight his work may appear to be; second, this technical skill and this intellectualism are only the superficies of his art. To recognize them certainly adds to the interest of his pictures but their enjoyment still depends first of all on our ability to respond to them unanalytically.

Figure 18

Figure 19

In the picture he calls *Demon as Pirate* (Plate 143) there is much that can be pointed out in explanation: that the fish at the left is related to hieroglyphics or sign-symbols of the kind that might be found scratched in rocks everywhere from the American Indian's West to aboriginal Australia; that the little animals in the boat have the same character plus humorous overtones; that as pure line the pattern of the two boats and the demon connects the picture with certain oriental traditions. The composition could be gone into at some length—the ornamental subtlety of its color, the deft placement of the three flags, the forward swooping line of the demon, its echo in the movement of the harpoons, its stabilization by the masts and the figure in the small tublike boat. But in the long run no explanation of *Demon as Pirate* is going to explain the most important things about it. It is a vision and a dream, and our response to it depends finally upon associations we bring

to it from deep within ourselves, associations that we might be at a loss to define.

Of course, this is more or less true of every picture we see. It was true of Giorgione's *The Tempest*, with which we began this discussion. The difference is that *Demon as Pirate* has only the most tenuous relationship with the world we know and hence depends upon associations of the most personal and inward kind. It happens also to depend upon other associations of a highly cultivated kind ranging over the whole field of the arts. This does not mean that *Demon as Pirate* need be richer in its rewards than *The Tempest* or than a realistic picture for that matter. But it does mean that like all great fantastic or visionary art, Klee's intriguing work will have very special rewards for anybody to whom it is rewarding at all.

Something by way of epilogue may be in order now, at the conclusion of these twelve discussions. But it should be brief in words; most of

25

it should be said by a painting. Daumier's *The Print Collector* (Plate 144) makes an appropriate statement.

As a picture "of" something *The Print Collector* shows us an ordinary man pursuing a hobby. He is going through one of the portfolios of tens of thousands of miscellaneous prints that crowd Paris bookstalls. But he might be looking at pictures anywhere, and if we ponder one question, then the inner subject of *The Print Collector* becomes apparent. The question is, why do pictures interest this man?

Why do pictures exist at all? Why do people look at them, respond to them, grow to love some and to dislike others, argue about them, defend and attack them, collect them, explore them, starve to paint them, build museums to protect them, cross oceans to see them?

In another Daumier, *La Soupe* (*Figure 19*), human creatures devouring food with animal intensity become symbols of the cycle of birth, life, death, birth—bound to the soil, nourished by it, and returning to it.

The Print Collector speaks of man's other life. This ordinary man is not a human animal but a human being who thinks, wonders, and tries to explain. He is the creature who stopped being an animal and became a human being when it became necessary for him to explain to himself the existence of the world and to find a reason for his presence in it. He was rubbing this explanation with colored clays onto the walls of caves some thirty thousand years ago. He is still painting, and he will continue to paint as long as he continues to be a man.

This curious, unceasing activity of the artist and the unwavering fascination his images hold for everybody suggest another definition to be added to the ones that have served as an outline in this effort to discover what a painting is:

A painting is an answer to a question.

Notes on the Painters

Giorgione, about 1478-1510, Italian

133. THE TEMPEST, ABOUT 1508

Oil on canvas. Height 32¾". Gallery of the Academy, Venice

Giorgione is a mysterious figure. Virtually nothing is known about him, and in the paintings attributed to him there are further mysteries about the subject matter. It is known that he was born in Castelfranco, and it is generally believed that he studied under Giovanni Bellini in Venice at the same time as Titian. *The Tempest*, or *Soldier and Gypsy* as it is sometimes called, is one of only four paintings not seriously questioned as being his work. The other three are an early altarpiece called *The Virgin of Castelfranco*, an ambiguous subject called *Three Philosophers*, and *The Sleeping Venus*, which is believed to have been painted the year of Giorgione's death and finished by Titian. *The Concert* is sometimes attributed to Palma Vecchio. In spite of the briefness of his life and the small number of paintings known to be his, Giorgione was one of the most important figures in Venetian painting. He turned its direction toward the poetic, sensuous reverie that typifies it in the High Renaissance, although no other painter invested it with his dreamlike serenity.

William Blake, 1757-1827, British

134. THE ARCHANGEL RAPHAEL WITH ADAM AND EVE (illustration for *Paradise Lost*), 1808

Water color. Height 19½". Museum of Fine Arts, Boston

Blake is one of those artists who appear from time to time—independent of the art of his day, even running counter to it, creating his art from some reservoir of intense, personal emotion that puts him beyond the limits of any school or classification. He worked at a time when artists painting in the "grand manner" and didactic practitioners of academic classicism dominated painting, along with the usual horde of skillful but often superficial portrait painters who have always been so productive in England. Blake was none of these. It is difficult, as a matter of fact, to say exactly what he was. He drew very directly and obviously upon the Italian renaissance masters Raphael and Michelangelo for his figures, but resembled neither of them in spirit. He was a true genius in the sense of the word that means an individual of inexplicable natural powers of expression or invention that seem to come from nowhere, to depend upon no precedent, yet to be complete in themselves. He was virtually unknown until he was sixty years old. At that time a group of admirers who had been close to him for many years managed to secure for him commissions to illustrate the book of Job and *The Divine Comedy*. Today Blake's stature as a major artist is not disputed, but people have strong personal reactions to his art. His work is among the most sought after among bibliophiles, and many painters—particularly those who are also printmakers—all but deify him. But for others he seems extremely mannered and artificial. This is to be expected of an art that is so directly and so completely the expression, at an intensely personal level, of an eccentric.

Hieronymus Bosch, active by 1488—died 1516, Flemish

135. THE GARDEN OF EDEN and HELL (left and right wings of THE GARDEN OF EARTHLY DELIGHTS)

Oil on wood. Height 7'2½". The Prado Museum, Madrid

136. Detail from HELL

Bosch had an exceptional career as an international painter, being as famous in Italy and in Spain as he was in his native Flanders. The fantastic nature of his art would suggest that he was an eccentric person obsessed by visions, somewhat like Blake if you wish, but this was not so. The fantasies he painted were intellectual moralities. Although their sources have been only recently (and partially) discovered, it now begins to be apparent that he drew upon the treatises of obscure and esoteric religious philosophers as well as upon popular subjects of his day. He has always been a conspicuous painter—it is impossible not to stop in front of one of his paintings in a museum—but lately he has again become a major influence on painters, as he was in his own lifetime but ceased to be during the centuries when idealism and realism made his painting appear to be a rather isolated phenomenon. The revival of interest in his work is due to the double discovery that it is intellectually more complicated than it seems and that he anticipated surrealist fantasies.

Salvador Dali, born 1904, Spanish

137. APPARITION OF FACE AND FRUIT DISH ON A BEACH, 1938

Oil on canvas. Height 45". The Wadsworth Atheneum, Hartford

Dali is without question the most irritating painter who has ever deliberately cultivated a public personality through buffooneries. A few years ago every other picture magazine one picked up recounted his latest stunt. Recently, however, these shenanigans have become stale copy. Eventually it may be possible to look again at a painting by Dali as a painting, rather than as a sensational news piece. At the moment it is difficult to evaluate him objectively; he has made it impossible to separate the private world of his painting from his public personality. By any standard, however, he is an arresting craftsman, no matter to what use he puts his talent. His art has been further distorted because its novel and theatrical elements, well suited to arts of display, have been cheapened in spuriously surrealist imitations. His work has had a strong influence on commercial window dressing and on specialized advertising directed toward a sophisticated audience. Dali himself has designed theatrical sets and jewelry and has made short experimental films.

His early training in his native Spain was academic, and he has continued to observe its disciplines in paradoxical combination with morbid and pathological subject matter. He was disowned by the original surrealist group in Paris, partly because of his academic technique, partly no doubt because of personal squabbles and jealousies. In 1940 he came to live in the United States where he has addressed himself to a wide public.

Giorgio de Chirico, born 1888, Italian

138. THE ANGUISH OF DEPARTURE, 1913–14

Oil on canvas. Height 33½". The Albright Art Gallery, Buffalo

Chirico was a surrealist before the term was invented. Adopting the word "metaphysical" to describe his painting, he issued statements concerning it and his intentions that have become the basis for a prolific school of contemporary painting. His verbal rigamaroles do not always do credit to his art, and they certainly do not clarify it, if it needs clarifying. Actually, Chirico's art should not need much explanation; once it is accepted as dream or vision it exists, as it should, without explanation. He has worked in a variety of manners; his latest one rejects the world of fantasy, returning to extremely conventional subject matter conventionally painted.

Arnold Böcklin, 1827-1901, Swiss

139. ISLAND OF THE DEAD, 1880

Oil on wood. Height 29". The Metropolitan Museum of Art, Reisinger Fund, 1926

Böcklin is a Swiss painter whose great popularity during his lifetime has so diminished that one rarely sees any of his work besides *Island of the Dead*, of which he did several versions. Fashions in art frequently temporarily obscure a painter's reputation, and current fashions make Böcklin's art seem, with occasional exceptions, rather obvious and heavy-handed. But he was a painter of very great vigor and intensity, and there are some indications that his reputation may be emerging from eclipse.

Washington Allston, 1779-1843, American

140. THE FLIGHT OF FLORIMELL, 1819

Oil on canvas. Height 35¾". The Detroit Institute of Arts

Allston was born in South Carolina, went to Harvard, studied painting in England, continued to study in Paris and in Italy, and, when he finally came home and settled in Boston, became an important figure in American intellectual life, as much in literature as in painting. Although he is thought of primarily as a force in the romantic revival and as a painter of moods ranging from gentle reverie to nightmare and horror, he also did the usual religious and historical pictures that were the painter's stock-in-trade at that time.

Thomas Cole, 1801-1848, American

141. IN THE CATSKILLS, 1837

Oil on canvas. Height 39". The Metropolitan Museum of Art, gift in memory of Jonathan Sturges by his children, 1895

Cole was born in England, but America claims him as a painter, since his family brought him to this country when he was seventeen, and he became a leader among those painters who discovered American landscape as a romantic subject. He particularly interpreted it in its grandeur and wildness and went beyond them to invent landscapes of the most tempestuous and fantastic kind. But he also had a sensitive feeling for the poetic intimacy of landscape, as seen in *In the Catskills*. He is equally well known as a wood engraver, the capacity in which he began his professional life. Altogether, he was an artist of very considerable range and inventiveness, of great sensitivity often obscured from the casual observer by what may appear to be detailed, literal realism, or flamboyant, obvious allegory.

Henri Rousseau, 1844-1910, French

142. LANDSCAPE WITH CATTLE

Oil on canvas. Height 20¼". The Philadelphia Museum of Art, Louise and Walter Arensberg Collection

Rousseau is one of the most difficult of all painters to explain, as has already been made apparent in the text. Although all his life he remained a genuinely simple, naïve, and—to judge by some of his statements and actions—even an obtuse man, few painters demand more subtlety and sophistication from the observer.

A large group of his paintings show jungle scenes full of fantastic foliage, exotic figures, savage animals, strange birds. These are his most popular works, since the decorative foliage and the interest of the subject matter are readily acceptable to almost anybody. A simpler subject, *Landscape with Cattle*, was chosen for illustration in this portfolio because it is more difficult for most people to appreciate, because its small size permits reproduction without too much reduction, and because Rousseau's quality is sometimes revealed best by continued acquaintance with a picture, all explanations aside.

Rousseau's friends were the little people of the quarter where he lived; he remained one of them all his life, though in his later years he also knew the painters of the *avant-garde* (including Picasso) whose art was, in its intellectualism, the opposite of his own. "Instinctive" is a word not in much favor and too easy a one to fall back on when the character of a man's art is difficult to describe, yet one must fall back on it in Rousseau's case. He was an instinctive painter if ever there was one. Part of his appeal is that this makes him refreshing in an age when painting carries a burden of theory that sometimes stifles it.

Paul Klee, 1879-1940, Swiss

143. DEMON AS PIRATE, 1926

Gouache on paper. Height 11½". The Philadelphia Museum of Art, Louise and Walter Arensberg Collection

Klee is in the extraordinary position of being a major painter who has never painted a major picture. It is only in his total work that his scope and his meaning become apparent. Individually his pictures may be only charming and may seem—may even be—trivial. Yet each Klee painting one knows enriches all the others, until eventually the psychological penetration behind the individual fantasies is revealed. The quality is always specialized, but it is not as limited as it first appears to be.

Also, Klee's way of painting is the end development of his participation in the German school of expressionism that emerged before the First World War, of his contact with cubism while it was still developing, and of his study of such painters as Cézanne, Van Gogh, and other great innovators of the end of the nineteenth century. Merely to list these influences means nothing; the reader unfamiliar with them will see nothing more in Klee's art for knowing that these influences are a foundation for its originality, but to the student of contemporary painting Klee's art is richer because in it the ideas that formed these men and schools are seen in new mutations. In short, Klee is a painter who demands special knowledge, special sensitivities, and special acquaintance if he is to be more than merely entertaining, but something of his poetic quality comes through in *Demon as Pirate*.

It should be added that Klee was a member of the staff of the Bauhaus, founded after the First World War. This German school developed and disseminated throughout Europe and America new methods of teaching that have now become standard in most art schools.

Honoré Daumier, 1808-1879, French

144. THE PRINT COLLECTOR

Oil on wood. Height 13⅜". The Philadelphia Museum of Art, W. P. Wilstach Collection

Daumier made his living all his life as a cartoonist. His paintings were known to very few people during his lifetime; upon his death they were acquired by a syndicate that sold them for a fortune.

Daumier did some five thousand cartoons for the journals *La Caricature* and *La Charivari*. Actually, "cartoon" is an inadequate word for his benevolent satires on the fortunes and misfortunes of the Parisian bourgeoisie, his trenchant comments on manners and morals, his powerful condemnations of injustice and political corruption. His deepest concern is always with the dignity and nobility of human life. In this respect his closest counterpart is Rembrandt, whose drawings and paintings influenced Daumier and are reflected in his fully developed style. As Rembrandt revealed human dignity in faces ravaged by time and poverty, so Daumier revealed it in the most commonplace, the most ordinary men. Even in his humorous cartoons, where all the pretensions and absurdities of the bourgeoisie are hilariously exposed, Daumier is never malicious. No matter how clearly he may see a little man's shortcomings, Daumier respects him as part of the mass of humanity that is ultimately good. But when humanity is violated by tyrants, by opportunists, or by stupid men in high places, he is merciless.

Daumier is one of the great draughtsmen of his century. In drawings composed of a few bent lines and quick wash of shadow he captures the structure of a head and with it the psychological identity of an individual. In a gesture, in an apparently casual attitude reduced to little more than a silhouette, he reveals the temperament, the social level, and the spirit of his subject, as he so brilliantly does in *The Print Collector*.